BEACH

BODY
art

BEACH
BODY art

AILEEN MARRON
in association with Halawa Henna

Photography by Emma Peios

JOURNEY
EDITIONS

'In all ages, far back into pre-history, we find human beings have painted and adorned themselves'

H. G. WELLS, *The Work, Wealth and Happiness of Mankind*

First published in the United States in 1999 by Journey Editions, an imprint of Periplus Editions (HK) Ltd., with editorial offices at 153 Milk Street, Boston, Massachusetts 02109.

The catalog card number is on file with the Library of Congress

ISBN 1-885203-77-2

DISTRIBUTED BY:

USA
Tuttle Publishing, Distribution Center
Airport Industrial Park
364 Innovation Drive
North Clarendon, VT 05759-9436
Tel: (800) 526-2778
Tel: (802) 773-8930

JAPAN
Tuttle Shokai Ltd.
1-21-13, Seki
Tama-ku, Kawasaki-shi
Kanagawa-ken 214-0022, Japan
Tel: (044) 833-0225
Fax: (044) 822-0413

First Edition
05 04 03 02 01 00 99   1 3 5 7 9 10 8 6 4 2

AN EDDISON•SADD EDITION
Edited, designed and produced by
Eddison Sadd Editions Limited
St Chad's House, 148 King's Cross Road
London WC1X 9DH

Phototypeset in Garamond ITC by BT and Geometric Slab BT
using QuarkXPress on Apple Macintosh.
Origination by Bright Arts PTE, Singapore
Printed and bound by C & C Offset Printing Co. Ltd, Hong Kong

page 20

page 24

page26

page 30

page 36

Contents

introduction

This book shows how to create ten diverse, ever-popular body-art designs. They are all based on traditional concepts while reflecting modern body art today.

I have focused these designs around a 'beach' theme – a great place to show off your creations – but the selection of motifs will appeal to everyone. There are also lots of stunning ideas to help you create your own designs and achieve your own personal style.

The beach expands your opportunities for body art: you have warm weather and are probably less covered up than usual. So experiment with designs in places, such as around your midriff, that, perhaps on a daily basis, wouldn't be on show. The beach is also a good place to apply designs while lounging in the sun – you could even create designs using the coloured sunblocks that are readily available. Remember that you can change your designs as often as you like as well as the body locations. You can also coordinate your body art with your clothing and the occasion. You'll find the different products used suit different occasions too.

history of body art

It is without a doubt human nature to express ourselves through various types of body art. For thousands of years, people from all over the world have decorated their bodies, with various forms of art becoming more fashionable in different regions at different times. For example, in the West, most women wouldn't dream of going out without their make-up, whilst

... in India consider their tattoos
... part of daily life.

...earching body art on a daily basis
through my work, I've noticed many parallels
in design across the world, looking at just
what, where and how body art is applied. As a
general rule, wherever the climate is gentler
on the human body you'll find that body art is
more popular. In the South Seas, for example,
where the climate is very warm, you'll find
traditional tattoos covering a lot of the body.
In the Middle East, on the other hand,
although the climate is
warm, most women keep
well covered up due
partially to religious
beliefs but also
because of the
very strong sunlight.
Hence, the most common
traditional form of body
art is applied in henna to
the hands and feet. In
parts of the world where
the weather is a lot
cooler, the major traditional form
of body art is make-up, as people spend the
greater part of the year covered up with only
their faces exposed.

Polynesian tattoos often cover much of the body

getting started

There are many products you can use for temporary body art. In this book I look at traditional henna, body paints, cosmetic inks and dyes, and show you the techniques you will need to get the very best effects from each. All these products are easy to get hold of *(see Useful Contacts, page 62)*.

Take a look at the ten designs in the book. They may look intricate, but can all be broken down into simple, repetitive steps. Select the medium you will use and try out the techniques demonstrated *(see pages 12–19)*. Start off with one of the simpler designs early in the book, like the Japanese calligraphy *(see pages 24–5)* which naturally lends itself to simple brushstrokes. Many of the designs have transfers which will give you something to follow and help you on your way. As you progress, move on to the more complex freehand designs later in the book, and try mixing and matching products, too. The design outlines are clearly shown for you to copy out. You can always skip the tricky bits until you get more practice. Remember – the designs are up to you. You can just copy them as they are, or copy elements of one design and add your own freehand motifs, or perhaps combine patterns from two different designs. The possibilities are endless!

Before you know it you will be mastering the techniques and designing your very own temporary tattoos. So call your friends round and get practising on each other straight away!

henna techniques

Henna body art uses a long-lasting and natural product. Fashionable in the East for thousands of years, it has finally made it to the West. Follow the preparation instructions with your henna (see Useful Contacts, page 62, for suppliers). Once prepared, henna paste is most effectively applied by piping it onto the skin, as you would squeeze icing through a tube. Henna stains the skin permanently, the design disappearing as the body regenerates its epidermis, about every 2–4 weeks. Henna will stain the skin a reddish-brown colour (the exact shade varies). *(For more information on henna, see Further Reading, page 63.)*

Catalyst solution is mixed with the henna powder

Henna powder

Mehlabiya oil is applied to the skin first to aid henna development

don't forget!

- Cleanse skin first and apply mehlabiya oil
- Leave design uncovered until dry
- Wait another hour before brushing off dry paste
- Don't get design wet for 12 hours
- Design takes 48 hours to develop full colour
- Design lasts 2–4 weeks

fine lines ▶

Holding the cone near the tip, squeeze the henna onto the skin. Use even pressure for an even line. Drag the tip across the skin from side to side, or from top to bottom as needed, moving the cone away from the direction of the flow of henna paste.

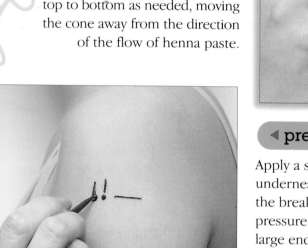

◀ pressure

Apply a small line with a dot underneath, then repeat this without the break, gradually increasing the pressure on the cone as you reach the large end. You can also start at the large end and work backwards.

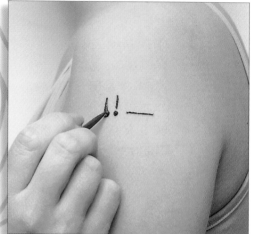

block fill ▶

Use rows of straight lines to fill in large areas. Remember that it is only the paste in contact with the skin that will stain, but don't worry about build-up on the skin – it is unavoidable. Don't try to spread product on the skin – you will remove more than you spread!

body-paint techniques

There are two main types of body paints available: grease and water-based. Both come in an array of colours. You don't need to keep adding water to grease paints, so they are quite quick to use, making them popular in theatres and with face painters. I like water-based paints more, though. I find application smoother and I like the fact that you can wash them off clothes! You can achieve a great number of effects with body paints, from basic backgrounds to detailed designs.

Grease body paints

Cosmetic sponges for blending paint

Water-based body paints

Paintbrushes in a range of sizes

don't forget!

- Cleanse skin first
- Set paint with talcum powder
- Use warm water and soap to remove water-based paints
- Use cleanser or baby oil to remove grease paints
- Designs last about 1 day

fine lines ▷

Using just a little body paint on the tip of a brush, rest your hand on the arm and apply a smooth line. Use the length of the brush as a guide for your line. When painting a long line, apply a small section at a time to keep control.

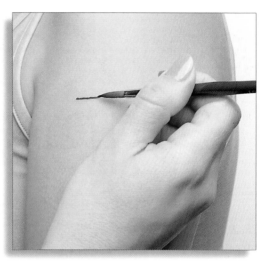

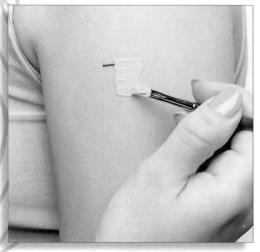

◁ block fill

Body paints dry very quickly, so you can apply a different colour over the first almost immediately. You can also apply a light colour over a dark one, so you don't have to plan the order of colour application. If you're filling in a large area, load your brush quite well.

texture ▷

You can create great paint effects using wet and dry sponges. Try applying wet paint in circular motions for a smooth background, or dabbing and smudging on finishing touches with a dry sponge – as I have here, with a shimmering silver.

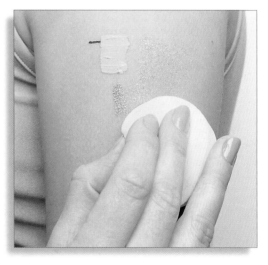

body-dye techniques

Cosmetic dyes can be hard to find in the shops. *(See Useful Contacts, page 62 to locate a good source.)* The dyes used in this book have been specially formulated to act like henna paste. However, Mother Nature is still the best because these coloured dyes last for 2–4 days, unlike henna which is a longer lasting cosmetic dye. Dying the skin creates the most realistic tattoo effect: no product is left on the skin, so there is no light reflection and hence detection.

Activator must be applied to the skin first

Body dyes come is a wide range of colours

Paintbrush for shading effects

don't forget!

- First cleanse skin and apply activator liquid
- Peel off dye when dry
- Designs last 2–4 days (waterproof spray will prolong their life)
- Remove with warm water and soap – will take about 7 washes

shading ▶

The gel-like dye can be mixed on the skin during application. Here I applied a yellow circle and then mixed blue directly into the still-wet product, gradually adding less blue as I neared the top left. After drying, the colour will gradually fade from yellow through to dark green.

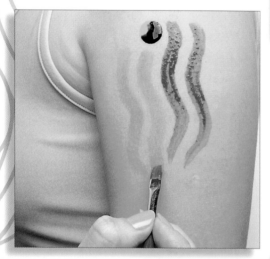

◀ brush work

Dyes can also be applied using a brush. Paint it on in its gel form, or water it down in a palette to paint lighter shades of the same colour. Here I've applied the product in gel form and *(far left)* in a very diluted form, illustrating the shading capabilities.

pressure ▶

Follow the henna instructions *(see page 13)*. Dye doesn't need as much pressure to force it out of the cone though. Once the product has dried (20–40 minutes), use your hand to gently rub the dry film away, revealing the temporary stain beneath.

cosmetic-ink techniques

All of us have used ink to draw on ourselves at sometime, whether just jotting down a phone number, or creating masterpieces as children. You must make sure, though, that you use a cosmetic ink (also known as temporary tattoo paint). The skin is a living organ and I recommend that all products you use on it are designed for the purpose. There are lots of cosmetic pens and inks available. Personally, I prefer the alcohol-based bottled inks that you apply with a brush. They dry very quickly and leave a clean edge (I find the 'felt-tip' kind tend to let the colour bleed around the edges of a design).

Alcohol-based cosmetic inks

Paintbrushes in a range of sizes

don't forget!

- Cleanse skin first
- Set ink with talcum powder
- Inks are waterproof – you need alcohol swabs or oil-based cleansers to remove them
- Designs will last 2–5 days

fine lines ▶

Use a fine brush, and follow the same instructions as when using body paint *(see page 15)*. You will need to keep an alcohol-based cleanser close at hand to keep the tip of your brush clean and free from residual product build-up.

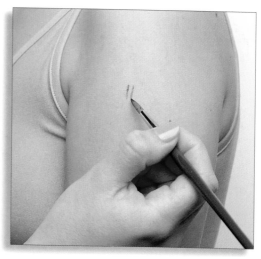

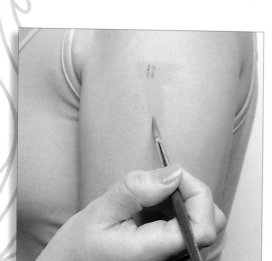

◀ block fill

Again, follow the instructions on page 15. You'll notice that a lighter-coloured ink will not cover a darker one, but will change colour slightly according to the colour applied on top. Here the fine blue lines now appear green.

mixing ▶

You can achieve some great effects if you mix colours on the skin. These inks are quite fast-drying, so you have to be quick and confident. I applied yellow from a loaded brush and then almost immediately began to add blue in vertical streaks.

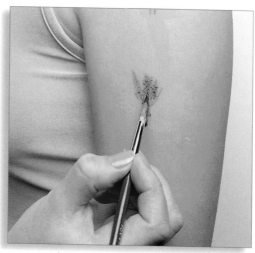

filigree garter

A *delicate design created in simple repetitive stages*

Natural henna is used here for a subtle and long-lasting design. It takes time to develop, but will last 2–4 weeks – ideal for a beach holiday! The complete design is continuous and free flowing, but it is easy to apply because you just repeat one section around the leg. Remember not to get the design wet for 12 hours after application.

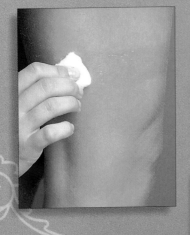

◀ one

Using cotton wool or a brush, apply a thin layer of mehlabiya oil to the skin. Cover the entire area of the design so the transfer leaves a good print and to ensure good colour development of the henna.

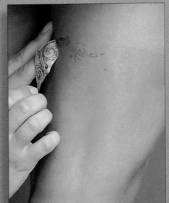

◀ two

Cut out the transfer, cutting right up to both ends of the central line. Now press the transfer firmly, ink-side down, against the skin with one hand. Use the other hand to peel it away.

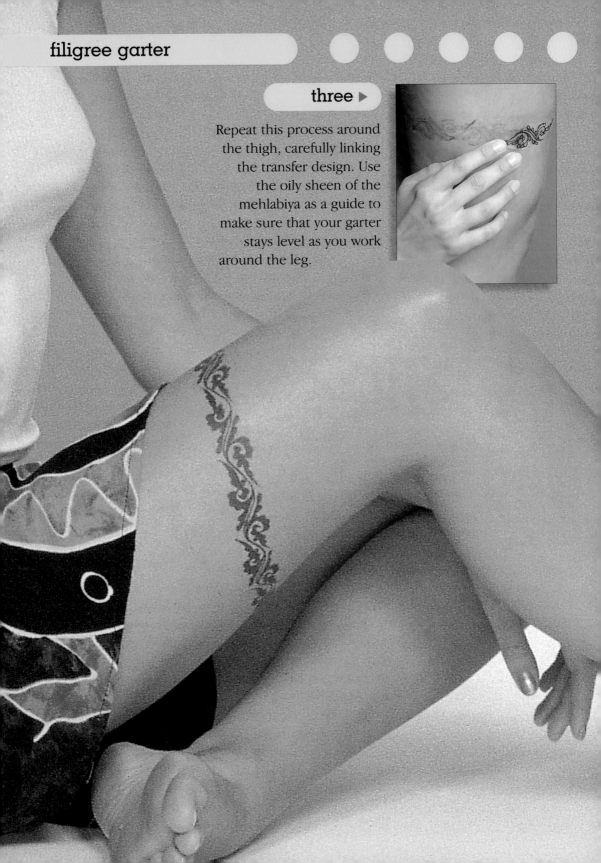

three ▶

Repeat this process around the thigh, carefully linking the transfer design. Use the oily sheen of the mehlabiya as a guide to make sure that your garter stays level as you work around the leg.

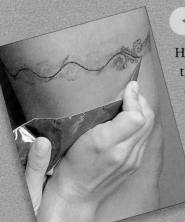

◀ four

Holding the henna cone near the tip, start to apply the central line of the design. Begin at the left-hand side and work around the leg, to avoid smudging the henna as you go. (Work right to left if you are left-handed.)

five ▶

Now go back to the start and fill in the details above and below the line. Again working from left to right, fill in the shapes using the pressure technique *(see page 13)*.

▼ six

Leave uncovered until completely dry (20–40 minutes). An hour after this, brush off remaining paste, revealing an orange design – full colour will develop over 48 hours.

Japanese calligraphy

Write your own message in just a few simple brushstrokes

Ever-popular, oriental calligraphy looks stunning in black cosmetic ink. It's easy to copy; just view the designs as a collection of short brushstrokes. To remove the inks you need alcohol swabs or baby oil, as they are not water-soluble – which makes them great for swimming!

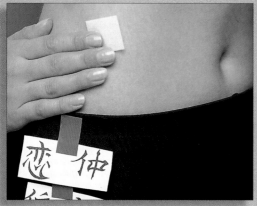

◄ one

Cleanse the skin with an alcohol swab to remove any natural oils that could prevent the ink taking. Then hold (or tape) your reference designs as close as possible to the area you are going to apply the designs to.

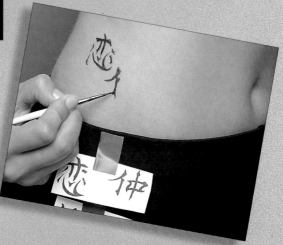

two ►

Tackle the designs in stages, painting one line at a time. Don't worry if you make a mistake: you can use an alcohol swab to remove any errors.

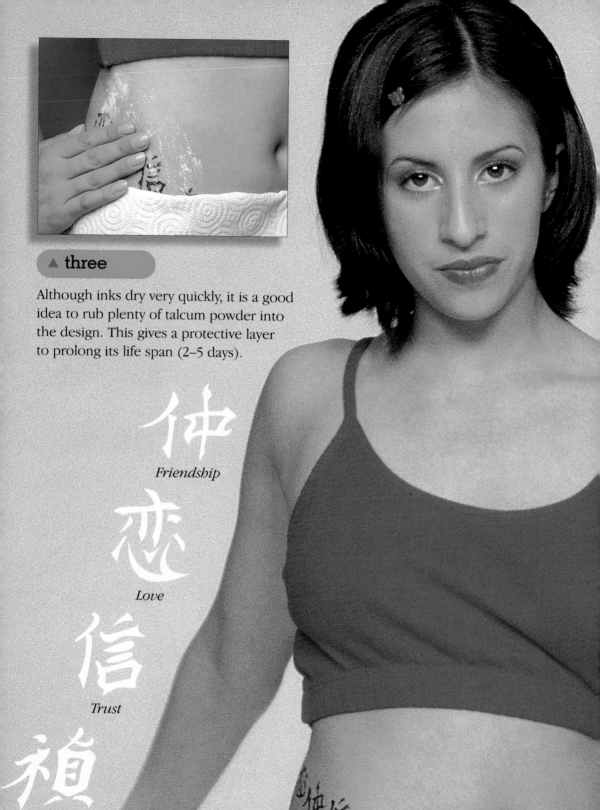

Although inks dry very quickly, it is a good idea to rub plenty of talcum powder into the design. This gives a protective layer to prolong its life span (2–5 days).

仲
Friendship

恋
Love

信
Trust

禎
Good Luck

circling dolphins

Combine two painting techniques for the ultimate water-babe look

Body paints have been used for this swirly design. Dolphins are fantastic animals to paint – they look great circling the navel, with or without this watery background.

▲ one

Use a well-loaded brush to apply white paint around the navel. Paint using large circular motions. The spiralling effect will help the colour effect illustrated in the next steps.

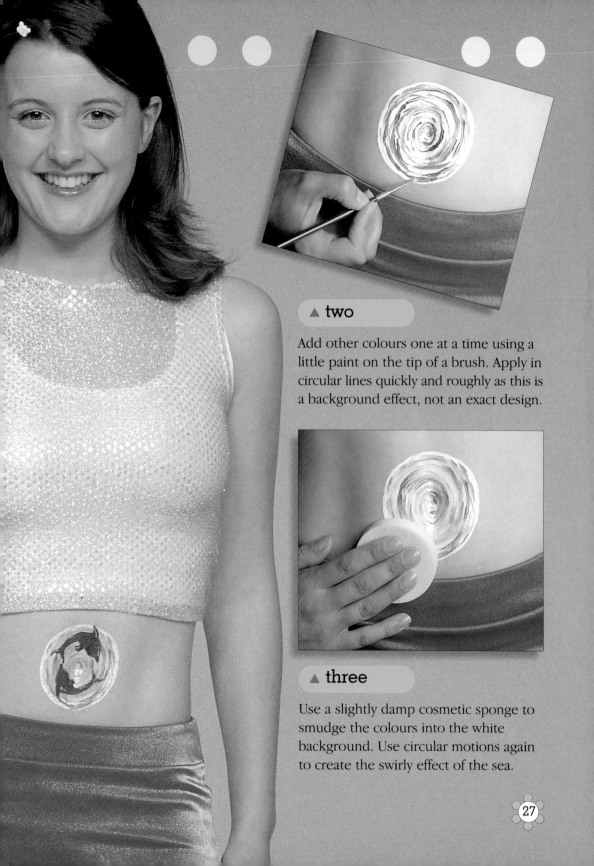

▲ **two**

Add other colours one at a time using a little paint on the tip of a brush. Apply in circular lines quickly and roughly as this is a background effect, not an exact design.

▲ **three**

Use a slightly damp cosmetic sponge to smudge the colours into the white background. Use circular motions again to create the swirly effect of the sea.

◄ four

Whilst the paint is still slightly damp, press the dolphin transfer, ink-side down, onto the background above the navel, then gently peel it away. Repeat with the transfer under the navel.

five ►

Using a tiny amount of paint on the tip of your brush, start to fill in the dolphins. Start with the top dolphin, working from left to right, painting a small section of outline and then filling in as you go.

◄ six

To really 'lift' your design, use a metallic-look paint to add a few highlights to your dolphins. Again, only use a tiny amount of paint on the tip of a brush. Apply some talcum powder to set the design.

29

stylized armband

A radiant centrepiece, sure to have a dazzling effect

Cosmetic dyes have been used here to create a very realistic tattoo effect. The centrepiece of the design is based on the sun and looks great with or without a band. Most of the design uses freehand symmetrical techniques, but a central transfer is included to set up the design.

one ▶

Apply a generous coating of activator *(see page 16)* to the skin and vigorously rub it in. Make sure you cover the entire area where you are going to apply the design.

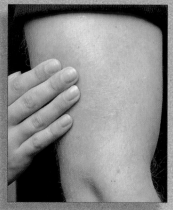

◀ two

Firmly press the central transfer onto the skin and then peel it away, leaving a design outline on the skin.

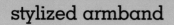

three ▶

Start to apply the cosmetic dye, filling in the teardrop shapes and dots inside the circle. Then apply dye over the circle outline, and follow this with a second circle.

▲ four

Apply a broken circle around the second circle, using it as a guide. To add the eight rays evenly, start with the top one and then apply the opposite one at the bottom. Repeat this with the other rays.

◄ five

When the gel has dried, peel it away from the skin. This is to prevent the black colour 'bleeding' into the yellow dye applied in the next step.

◀ six

Fill in the centre of the circle with yellow dye, avoiding the black shapes. Then fill in the ring between the two black circles, followed by the surrounding rays.

seven ▶

Using both colours, apply large teardrops alternately around the arm using the pressure technique *(see page 13)*. Mark a navy dot between each teardrop.

eight ▶

Finish off the armband by applying dots in alternate colours, zig-zagging through the teardrops.

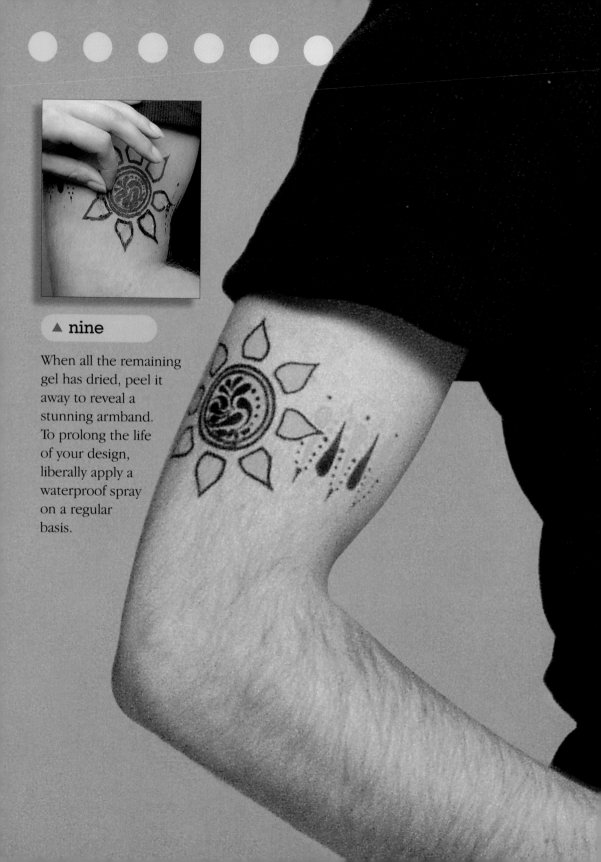

▲ nine

When all the remaining gel has dried, peel it away to reveal a stunning armband. To prolong the life of your design, liberally apply a waterproof spray on a regular basis.

Eastern foot design

Be first off the mark with freehand henna skills

This beautiful traditional foot design uses natural henna. It is a combination of Arabic and Indian style: the strong festoons circling the sole and the designs on the toes are Arabic, whilst the more intricate design on top is Indian. The combination is stunning.

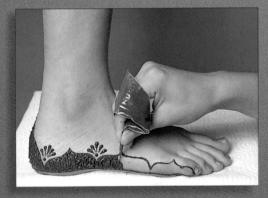

▲ one

Apply mehlabiya oil all over the foot. Then, holding the henna cone near the tip, apply the outline of the festoon. Then fill in these shapes and apply the flowers, starting with the dot and then the five teardrops.

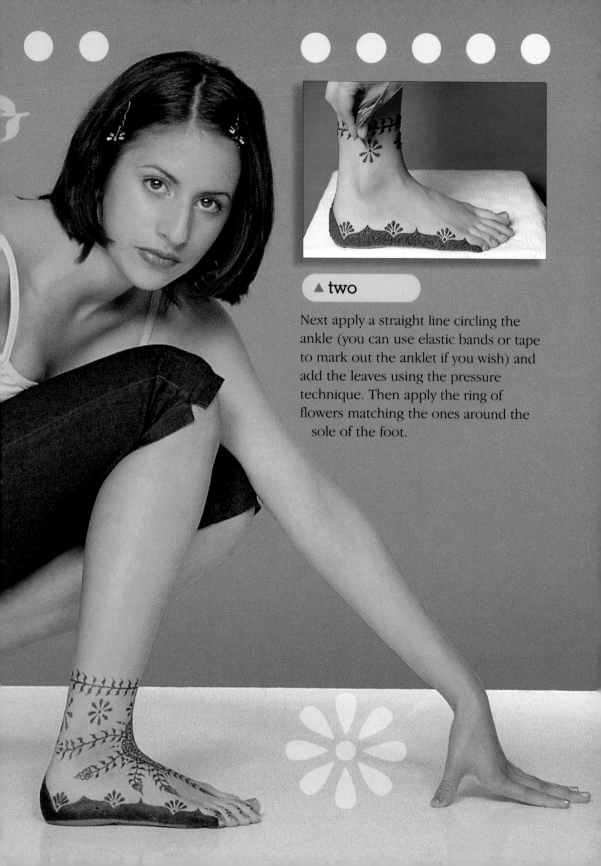

Next apply a straight line circling the ankle (you can use elastic bands or tape to mark out the anklet if you wish) and add the leaves using the pressure technique. Then apply the ring of flowers matching the ones around the sole of the foot.

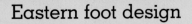

three ▶

Apply the central leaf transfer to the top of the foot. Outline it and fill in the details. Next outline this leaf with a thicker line. Surround this with teardrops, topping it off with a teardrop flower. Finally, outline this shape with a double line, add short lines in between and scalloping at the top *(see below opposite)*.

▼ four

Start at the top of the central design and apply the free-flowing tendrils as you did with the initial ankle bracelet *(see pages 36–7)*. Finish each branch with a heart-shaped leaf, outline it and add the details.

five

Now apply the toe designs. Start at the base of the nail with a dot and then apply the teardrops to build up flowers as before. Finish off with another dot and teardrop along the toe. Leave to dry completely and then wait another hour before brushing off the henna. Allow 48 hours for the colour to develop.

Japanese dragon

Hit the beach with this colourful and vibrant ink design

This design is based on traditional Japanese shoulder tattoos and has been created using cosmetic inks. The background is applied freehand, but transfers are used for the dragon's head and flower outlines.

▲ one

Cleanse the area with an alcohol swab and paint two spirals onto the skin using black ink. Then, starting at the centre of the spirals, paint on the semi-circles. Use the tip of the brush for greater control.

40

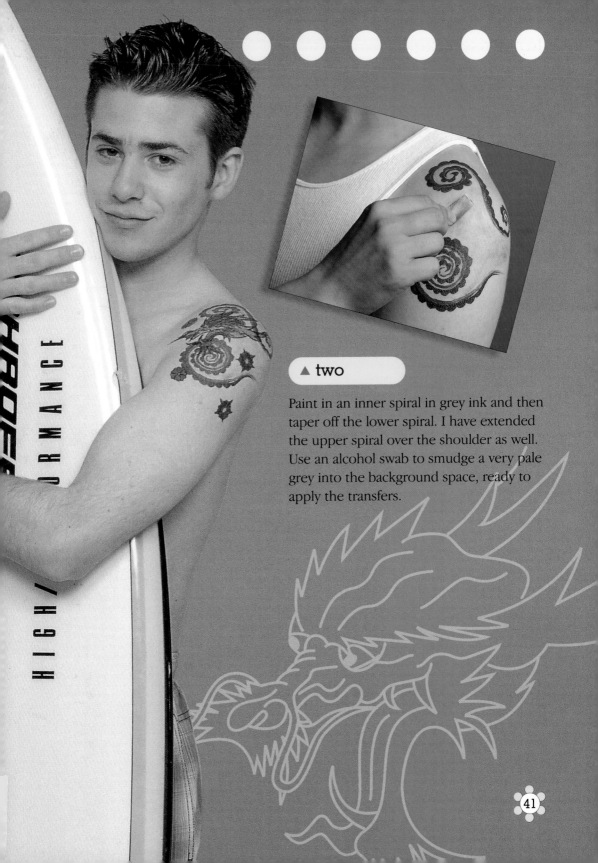

▲ **two**

Paint in an inner spiral in grey ink and then taper off the lower spiral. I have extended the upper spiral over the shoulder as well. Use an alcohol swab to smudge a very pale grey into the background space, ready to apply the transfers.

◀ three

While the skin is still wet with alcohol, firmly press the dragon's head transfer, ink-side down, onto the skin. Don't worry if some of the transfer goes over the background.

four ▶

Apply the flower transfers randomly around the design – wetting the skin with alcohol first. Next paint over the dragon outline in black, then fill in the colours – I've used green as the main colour here.

◀ five

Outline and paint in the flowers. You can always add more flowers or background swirls if you wish.

six ▶

Liberally apply and rub in talcum powder to make sure the design is dry and to set it. This is now quite waterproof and ready for the beach!

Borneo star

Follow these simple stages – and try adding a few of your own

Water-based body paints have been used to create this tattoo from Borneo. Traditionally it is placed on the front of a man's shoulder, but the design is so strong it looks great anywhere. Using the transfer from the Stylized Armband *(see page 30)* will help get you started.

◀ **one**

Use the transfer to give you a circle outline for the centre of this design. Cleanse the skin and, while it is still damp, press the transfer, ink-side down, against the skin.

◀ two

Using a small amount of black paint on the tip of a brush, paint over the outline of the circle. Next paint on eight lines radiating from the circle. Paint the lines that are opposite each other to guarantee symmetry, first the top vertical line and then the lower one, and so on.

three ▶

Paint rounded-tip triangles onto the design: the widest part of the triangle connecting with the circle and the tip being the end of the lines applied in the last step. Next, paint in another series of radiating lines, much shorter than the previous ones, originating in the indents between the triangles. Paint rounded-tip triangles onto these lines as well.

◀ four

Using a well-loaded brush, apply white paint to the central circle, paying close attention to the circumference. Don't worry if you paint white into the black because you can always repaint black over it.

◀ five

Using black paint again, start in the centre of the white circle and paint on the wave-like spiral. Apply talcum powder to the design to set it.

◀ six

It's easy to customize this design. Here I simply painted over the centre circle with gold and then added the black details. Experiment with different outlines too, like the ones above and opposite.

tribal rose collar

Who needs jewellery when simple shading can achieve this stunning collar piece?

This design is based on traditional European rose tattoos. I have used some basic tribal designs to liven up the roses and to 'fit' the design to the body, working along the collarbone and following the neckline of the dress. Try customizing it to wear on the lower back or stomach.

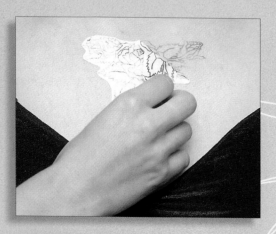

▲ **one**

Rub activator into the skin, covering the entire area of the design. Firmly press the transfer against the skin, and then peel away.

48

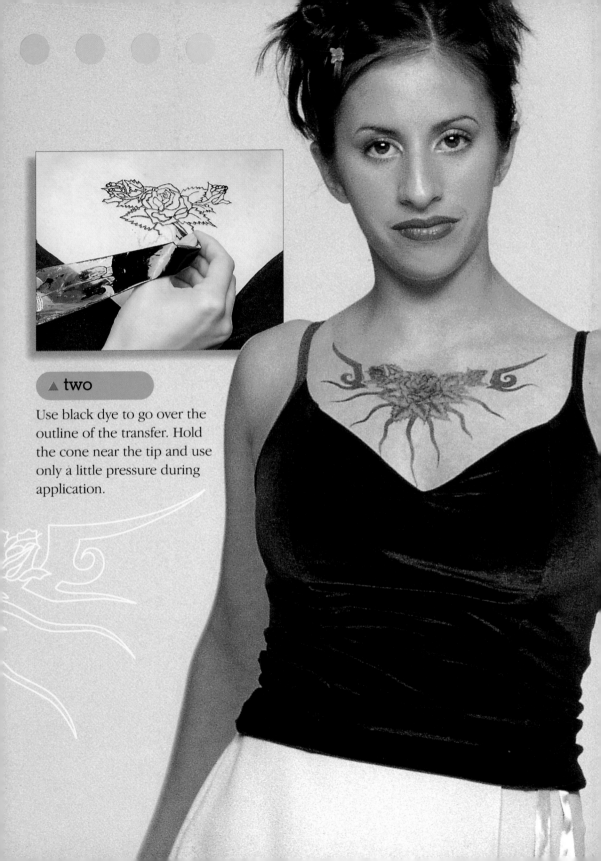

▲ **two**

Use black dye to go over the outline of the transfer. Hold the cone near the tip and use only a little pressure during application.

▲ three

Now take a deep red dye to
fill in most of the roses.
Leave some of the petals
so that you can use a
lighter colour to achieve
a good shading effect.

Use dark green to fill in the centre of the leaves. Again leave some of the leaves clear, ready to apply a lighter colour.

five ▶

Fill in the rest of the roses with an orange dye. Use the tip of your cone to blend the dyes where they meet. Next apply some yellow dye to the leaves. Then, using the green again, fill in the rest of the leaves and blend the dyes where they meet.

◀ six

To finish off the design, use the black again and add some freehand tapering trails and tribal shapes, securing the design to the collarbone. Let the product dry and then peel off *(see page 17)*, revealing the end result – a realistic, classic tattoo design.

Celtic lizard

These gold flecked effects look great on sun-kissed skin

A combination of cosmetic inks and body paints have been used to create this fabulous design. The paints have been used to build up the colour of the lizard, whilst the ink has been used to paint in the Pictish (early Celtic) design of the lizard. This versatile design also looks great climbing around the ankle.

◀ one

Use a brush well loaded with paint to mark on a very rough lizard shape, a little larger than the transfer size. Next 'dab' on lots of silver, gold and bronze dots to create a slightly scaly effect.

two ▶

Whilst the body paint is still damp, press the lizard transfer onto the skin, then peel it away gently.

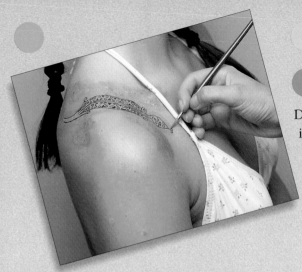

◀ three

Dip the tip of a brush into black cosmetic ink and simply paint over the transfer lines on top of the body paint.

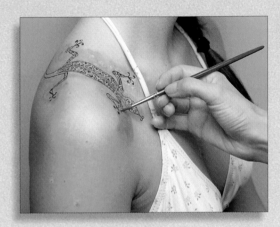

◀ four

Complete the lizard by copying the legs onto the body. Next, clean up the edges of the around the lizard using cotton wool and soapy water or a cleanser, depending on the type of paints you are using *(see page 14)*.

five ▶

Now add tiny amounts of orange onto the lizard's toes and eyes to enhance it. Finally apply talcum powder liberally to set the design.

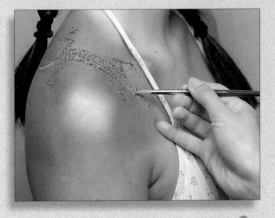

Indian bracelet

Don't be daunted by this intricate design – just follow the interlocking, repetitive stages

Natural henna and cosmetic dyes have been used to create this elaborate design incorporating traditional Indian motifs that are usually applied to the hands and feet.

one ▶

Apply mehlabiya oil to the wrist. Holding the henna cone near the tip, start with the central dot of the flower. Outline it, then add the eight teardrops. Next outline these and then outline the flower. Apply the curled lines and dots, setting the lines into the indents in the flower outline.

◀ two

Surround these shapes with leaf-shaped outlines, then apply a second line around the leaves. Next create the filled-in leaf shapes by applying teardrops with the wide end set in the indents between the leaves. Finally outline the solid leaves.

Indian bracelet

three ▶

Surround the entire design with a series of semi-circle outlines, creating a scalloped effect. Next add curls to the tip of each leaf.

◀ four

Apply teardrops to the tips of the pattern and outline them, taking care at this point not to rest your hand on the rapidly growing design and smudge it.

five ▶

Apply the widest line around the wrist first. Start with a sketchy line and then even it out: the width of the line allows leeway for error. Use this line as a guide when applying the narrower lines above and below it.

Indian bracelet

six ▶

Apply the series of curls to the upper narrow line and then follow the shapes with a double outline. As you work around the wrist, also apply the triangles to the other narrow line and fill in with smaller, solid triangles inside.

◀ **seven**

Apply solid triangles set into the indents in the curved (upper) border. Outline these and add the semi-circular scallop detail *(see step three)*, then the curls, three leaves and central dot to each point. On the other side of the band, add the teardrops to the tips of the triangles. Outline these and add the semi-circles.

eight ▶

Now take an orange cosmetic dye to fill in all the remaining spaces in the flower. Most of the henna will be dry by now, but be careful not to smudge any that isn't.

nine ▲

Finish off by filling in the rest of the band. Leave the design to dry for about an hour (to ensure henna colour development) and then remove both products by rubbing and brushing. The whole design will appear orange at first, but keep it dry for the first 12 hours and the henna will develop to a rich brown in 48 hours.

Useful contacts

Established in 1993, Halawa Henna Ltd are the original manufacturers and suppliers of retail and professional henna body art products. Halawa Henna run training courses for professionals and enthusiasts, and now supply a wide range of unique temporary body art products alongside henna. All the products used in this book are available by mail order from Halawa Henna. For further information, contact Halawa Henna Ltd, UK – or a Halawa Henna distributor closer to home. For up-to-date information on products, supply or your nearest professional artist, contact Halawa Henna at the address below or visit their website at www.hennatattoos.com.

UNITED KINGDOM
Halawa Henna Ltd
96–98 Chapel Street, Leigh
Lancashire WN7 2DB
Tel: (44) 01942 709906
UK freephone 0800 7311160
Fax: (44) 01942 709901
Email: enquires@hennatattoos.com

UNITED STATES
HALAWA HENNA PROFESSIONAL AND
RETAIL DISTRIBUTION
Kathy Rudy
Koolsville, 2639 West Lincoln Avenue
Anaheim, California 92801
Tel: (562) 866 8741
Email: katzkool@aol.com

AUSTRALIA
HALAWA HENNA MAIL-ORDER
DISTRIBUTION
Sandra Ongley
Taking Care of Business
34 Faukland Crescent
Kings Park, 2148 NSW
Tel/Fax: (02) 9837 3100

NEW ZEALAND
HALAWA HENNA PROFESSIONAL AND
RETAIL DISTRIBUTION
Andrew Arkwright
Dome New Zealand
717 Manukau Road, Auckland
PO Box 24   165
New Zealand
Tel/Fax: (09) 625 4921

OTHER SUPPLIERS
A wide range of products is available in high
street stores, but always check that the
products are designed to be used on the skin.
Look for an ingredients listing – if there isn't

one, don't buy the product. Patch test any
product first, especially if you have sensitive
skin. Body paints and inks are readily available
from theatre make-up stores, such as:

CHARLES FOX, 22 Tavistock Street, Covent
Garden, London WC2E 7PY, UK
Tel: 0171 240 3111

KRYOLAN has outlets throughout the United
States. Contact them at the address below for
your nearest stockist.
KRYOLAN CORPORTATION, 132 Ninth
Street, San Francisco, CA 94103.
Tel (415) 863 9684

Further reading

*If you're looking for more
inspiration to create your
own designs, try some of
these books – they're
crammed full of ideas to
help you expand your skills.*

Marron, Aileen. *Celtic Body
Art*. Boston, MA: Journey
Editions, 1999. Toronto: élan
press, 1999. London:
Piatkus, 1999. Sydney:
Simon & Schuster, 1999

Marron, Aileen. *The Henna
Body Art Kit*. Boston, MA:
Journey Editions, 1998.
Toronto: élan press, 1998.

London: Piatkus, 1998.
Sydney: Simon & Schuster,
1998

Richie, Donald and Ian
Buruma. *The Japanese
Tattoo*. New York:
Weatherhill, 1995

Schiffmacher, Henk. *1000
Tattoos*. Köln, New York,
London, Tokyo: Taschen,
1996

Wroblewski, Chris. *Skin
Shows: The Art of Tattoo*.
Secaucus, NJ: Carol
Publishing, 1991

Wroblewski, Chris. *Skin
Shows II: The Art of Tattoo*.
Secaucus, NJ: Carol
Publishing, 1991

Wroblewski, Chris. *Skin
Shows III: The Art of Tattoo*.
Secaucus, NJ: Carol
Publishing, 1994. London:
Virgin, 1994

Wroblewski, Chris and Steve
Beard. *Skin Shows IV: The
Art of Tattoo*. New York:
London Bridge, 1996.
London: Virgin, 1995

ACKNOWLEDGEMENTS

AUTHOR'S ACKNOWLEDGEMENTS

I would like to thank Simon Finley, Neil and Wendy Madgwick and Donna Morris for all their support and help, and for putting up with me whilst writing this book!

Thanks to everyone at Eddison Sadd Editions Limited for making it happen, especially Elaine Partington, Liz Wheeler, Tessa Monina, Sophie Bevan and Jamie Hanson, without whose excessive hard work and support this book would not have been possible, and of course the creative talents of Emma Peios.

Extra special thanks to Jeanette and Tony Finley, and Pat and Keith Marron (Mum and Dad), for their on-going support and hard work, and without which Halawa Henna Limited would not exist.

PICTURE CREDITS

The photograph on pages 8–9 is reproduced by kind permission of Chris Wroblewski.

EDDISON • SADD EDITIONS

Art Director Elaine Partington
Senior Art Editor Jamie Hanson
Senior Designer Marissa Feind
Commissioning Editor Liz Wheeler
Editor Sophie Bevan
Proofreader Michele Turney
Photographer Emma Peios
Line artworks Anthony Duke
Production Karyn Claridge and Charles James